Te amo larry nunca me
dejes o no se que aria en
mi vida estoy loca por ti
mi amor Att: tu chiquita que
te ama con todo tu corazon
quiero que me hagas el amor

12.4.08   AIRPORT ST. MARTIN

CHOICES, EACH MINUTE HOUR / DAY / WEEK . . . . ,
= YEAR = DECADE = LIFETIME

THINK CONCIOUSLY !

Architect   Architect   FOOL AROUND WITH THIS
Architect   Architect   LETS GET
Architect   Architect   GRAPHICALLY CREATIVE.
             Architect   . . . . THAT'S WHAT IT'S
                          ALL ABOUT. —
                          EXPAND HORIZONS ⟵ ⟶

c W   COLORS ALSO
      CR
      W   USE GOLD SMITH
               LOGO ?
                                                    AIA
Design Workshop   ENVIRONMENTAL   NCARB
                         ORNMENTAL   VI
                         SCULPTURAL   VA
IRUN APP FOR WORK ?   MA
                                                    MD

STARTING A NEW BOOK IS LIKE FACING
A BLANK CANVAS . . . . SPLASH SOME PAINT . . . .
BREAK THE INTIMIDATION ROAR OFF INTO IT.
LIKE LIFE . . . . . JUST START SOME WHERE
MID POINT, CORNER IT REALLY DOES NOT 'MATTER
WHAT MATTERS IS . . . . . . JUST JUMP IN ANY WHERE
AND START WITH OUT KNOWg WHAT MAY EVOLVE. ♡

THE OMNIVORE'S DILEMA   MICHAEL POLLAN
ANIMAL VEGETABLE MIRACLE   BARBARA KINGSOLVER

FAST FOOD NATION ?
PLENTY ?

DEPLETION & ABUNDANCE   SHARON ASTYK

DEEP ECONOMY.   BILL McKIBBON
PLAN B 2.0 (OR LATER)   LESTER BROWN
EATING FOSSIL FUELS: DALE PFEIFFER
  OIL & THE COMING CRISIS IN AGRICULTURE

THE SHOCK DOCTRINE   NAOMI KLEIN

REALLY FACINATING WOMAN
↑
I WONDER WHAT INDIA IS DOING THIS
VERY MOMENT ?   4·12·08   14:04   ?

I WANT TO HAVE FUN WITH LIFE.... TO LOOK
IT SQUARE IN THE EYE, ASK FOR WHAT I
WANT — TO SHAKE OFF THE CLOAK OF
MY FATHER .. TO LET OUT THE REAL ME

INSEL AIR, (CARIBBEAN JET.COM) 12.4.08 17:59
ENROUTE CURACAO
I WILL ARRIVE TO MAIVIS' BIRTHDAY PARTY
A DARLING WOMAN, IT WILL BE A GOOD
TIME WITH OLD FRIENDS & FAMILAR FACES.

TONIGHT I WILL LIGHT A CANDEL ABOARD
CARA MIA & GIVE THANKS TO BE "HOME AGAIN"
LAST TIME I CLEARED IN CUSTOMS, THE
INSPECTOR LOOKED AT ALL MY STAMPS AND
SAID "WELCOME HOME" TRULY A BEAUTIFUL,
FRIENDLY PLACE

I FORGOT MY "BOAT BOOKS" IN ANNAPOLIS SO
THE WORK LIST MAY START FROM SCRATCH OR
I MAY HAVE A "TO DO" LIST IN THE NAV. STATION
NO MATTER ..... THE BIG PROJECTS ARE OBVIOUS
MOST REPAIRS MADE UPON DEPARTURE AS ALWAYS.
THE EXHAUST STAND PIPE WOULD BE REBUILT HERE
IF I HAD TIME. HOPEFULLY THE MARINE TEX WILL
HOLD FOR A WHILE.

CREW ARRIVING SOON (MONDAY) ADDS THE
DIMENSION OF TIGHT QUARTERS. I NEED TO
COMPLETE ENG. SERVICE & HEAD SERVICE PRIOR TO
ARRIVAL.
HOPE IMKA CAN SELL MY NEW DINGHY.

12.7.08 LARRY'S FEST...
TACO SALAD -
BUSY BOAT DAY.
   INSTL — BIMINI, DODGER
        WIND INST + RIG CHECK   ALOFT
        SCRUB DECK, SOME METAL WORK
        SCRUB BELOW, MILDEW

        WORK W/ RUDY, MAIVIS BROTHER.
        NEW MAUI JIM GLASSES BROKEN
        MEDITATING BUT STILL HAVE ANXIETY
        MOMENTS —

YESTERDAY
IMKA - RENTAL CAR
        BUY NEW D4 BATTERIES.

        FEISTY - MEL + JACKIE ON DOCK
       CONSTANST - BURNED UP

            BARBARA & JOHN O'CONNOR,
            WHAT A SHOCK.

EVENING W/ PATRICIA.
    SNAK SHACK, BOOK OPENING
    FUN W/ HER - STILL FLASH BACK
    ON SON DAVID & HUSBAND TOM
    UPSET APPLE CART WITH JOHN
    OH S---

TODAY AGAIN — THOUGHTS OK J WHEN IT
COMES TO PASSAGEMAKING. MISS HER
BUT FEELING GOOD ABOUT THE BREAK
LOTS OF POTENTIAL EMAIL COMPANIONS
OUT THERE ON GREEN SINGLES. A GOOD
SWITCH — WE WILL SEE WHAT TRANSPIRES ??

I MISS MY BOAT BOOKS, IN ANNAPOLIS
   DID NOT PACK - FORGOT.
   RE: BOAT WORK LIST + PROVISION LIST.
   MAOOPS - MENTIONED THAT.

CREW ARRIVES TOMORROW, CRUNCH DAY.

12.10.08 , 7:25
ON DECK, CARA MIA , B ON A RUN, K&J SLEEP.
IMKA TO DAY W/ NEW BATTERIES
SOLD DINGHY , -10% , ENGINE TOO? NEW
TODAY OUT TO HARBOR. BOTTOM CLEAN, ZINC.
CHECK 2hp OUT BOARD. - CLEAN TOP SIDES.

EMAIL W/ INDIA, CATHERINE, BEACHGIRL
CONNECT W/ KEN, JVW, EDWARD S. , J

LAUNDRY , ORGANIZE VITS.
SITTING ON DECK W/ TEA, BEAUTIFUL MORNING.
GREAT DAY TO BE OUT SAILING!
CARA MIA , LOOKING PRETTY GOOD FOR AN OLD GIRL.

12.11.08. STOP, PAUSE,.... GIVE THANKS....
FOR THIS MOMENT! 06:49 AM SERU BOCA MARINA
SITTING IN COCKPIT CARA MIA, DAWN, SUN NOT YET
OVER THE HILL, JOHN, KENNA SLEEPING BRUCE GONE
FOR APPOINTMENT. THANKS FOR THE BOAT & SPECIALLY
THE CREW, WONDERFUL SOULS AS WE LEARN MORE
ABOUT EACH OTHER. EVERY DAY HAS BEEN A BIG
DAY. YESTERDAY WE INSTALLED TWO NEW D4 AGM
BATTERIES. HEAVY EVV... GOOD TO HAVE HELP & BE AT
THE DOCK. LATER BARBARA BEACH & BOTTOM SCRUB,
NEW ZINC & TOP SIDES SCRUB. DINNER W/ PATRICIA
AT THAI RESTURANT.
INDIA CHECKED IN WITH RECENT PHOTOS, INT. LIV. ARTICLE
ON BRASIL & A LONG EMAIL. A GOOD CHOICE FOR HER
BUT NOT ME. RIGHT BRAIN/LEFT HAND.. ME TOO BUT NO
LUCK W/ LANGUAGE. GOT A LITTLE SPARK FROM CW
CATHERINE (BELIZE) & BEACH GIRL MAY HAVE SCREWED
UP W/ DUMB EMAIL. SA LA VIE. GIVE J A TUNEIN,
EDWARD RE HOUSE. STU AGAIN W/ DEP DATE (NO WORD)
LAST EMAIL. —

12·13·08 ON BOARD CARA MIA, SOUTH COAST
CURACAO, 14:13 MOTOR W/ MAINSAIL ALONG
COAST TOWARD POINT KANON, GENTLE SEAS 2 FT. ±
LIGHT WIND, SCAT. CLOUDS, RUN FRIG. NICE START
OF VOYAGE TO ST. J. WOW CHANGES! "CONSTANCE"
BURNED & SUNK IN BONAIRE, AMERICAN SAILOR
SHOT, ISL. OFF PUERTO LA CRUZ, TONY EDWARDS
DIED SUDENLY. GIVE THANKS FOR GIFTS WE HAVE
AND THE MOMENT.

MAR 10 , LONG TIME , NO ENTRY , G.C. BAY
EARLY AM , EAGLES ON STERIO .... "TAKE IT EASY"
7 WOMEN ON MY MIND WOW! SLIGHT OVERLOAD
JOHN ET AL ARRIVE FRIDAY , BOAT NEEDS WORK.
ENG. OVERHEATING IS BIGGY , THEN B&G . PAM AT
OFFICE TO BULDOZE PAPER INTO FILES . NEED TO
MEASURE & ORDER OIL COOLER . GET SUPPLIES,
LINE UP DAVID IF POSS. LOTS TO DO HERE +
WORK / TAXES PREP etc. etc. , GINNY WAS A
SURPRISE WITH HER INVITATION TO FLA. INC.
MOM VISIT AS WELL ? MORE LATER , ...